Samuel French Acting Edition

Wild Goose Dreams

by Hansol Jung

SAMUELFRENCH.COM SAMUELFRENCH.CO.UK

ISBN 978-0-573-70804-6

www.SamuelFrench.com
www.SamuelFrench.co.uk

For Production Enquiries

United States and Canada
Info@SamuelFrench.com
1-866-598-8449

United Kingdom and Europe
Plays@SamuelFrench.co.uk
020-7255-4302

Each title is subject to availability from Samuel French, depending upon country of performance. Please be aware that *WILD GOOSE DREAMS* may not be licensed by Samuel French in your territory. Professional and amateur producers should contact the nearest Samuel French office or licensing partner to verify availability.

MUSIC USE NOTE

Licensees are solely responsible for obtaining formal written permission from copyright owners to use copyrighted music in the performance of this play and are strongly cautioned to do so. If no such permission is obtained by the licensee, then the licensee must use only original music that the licensee owns and controls. Licensees are solely responsible and liable for all music clearances and shall indemnify the copyright owners of the play(s) and their licensing agent, Samuel French, against any costs, expenses, losses and liabilities arising from the use of music by licensees. Please contact the appropriate music licensing authority in your territory for the rights to any incidental music.

IMPORTANT BILLING AND CREDIT REQUIREMENTS

If you have obtained performance rights to this title, please refer to your licensing agreement for important billing and credit requirements.

WILD GOOSE DREAMS was originally developed by the Public Theater in the Public Studio in New York City in April 2017. The production was directed by Leigh Silverman, with sets by Wilson Chin, costumes by Ntokozo Fuzunina Kunene, lighting by Brian Tovar, sound by Joanna Lynne Staub, music composition by Paul Castles, and Korean songs by Jongbin Jung. The production stage manager was Leigh Selting. The cast was as follows:

YOO NANHEE . . . . Sandra Oh
GUK MINSUNG . . . . James Yaegashi
FATHER . . . . Raul Aranas
MAN . . . . Marrick Smith
WOMAN . . . . Stacey Sargeant
HEEJIN . . . . Stephanie Hsu
WIFE . . . . Cindy Cheung
CHORUS . . . . Dan Domingues, Jessie Shelton, Britton Smith

WILD GOOSE DREAMS was first produced by the Public Theater in New York City in a co-production with La Jolla Playhouse in La Jolla, California.

The La Jolla production ran from September to October 2017. The performance was directed by Leigh Silverman, with sets by Wilson Chin, costumes by Linda Cho, lighting by Keith Parham, sound by Joanna Lynne Staub, music composition by Paul Castles, and Korean songs by Jongbin Jung. The production stage manager was Melanie J. Lisby. The cast was as follows:

YOO NANHEE . . . . Yunjin Kim
GUK MINSUNG . . . . James Kyson
FATHER . . . . Francis Jue
MAN . . . . Julian Cihi
WOMAN . . . . Carolyn Agan
HEEJIN . . . . Samantha Wang
WIFE . . . . Rona Figueroa
CHORUS . . . . DeLeon Dallas, Kyle Hester, Kimberly Monks

The New York production ran from October to December 2018. The performance was directed by Leigh Silverman, with sets by Clint Ramos, costumes by Linda Cho, lighting by Keith Parham, sound by Palmer Hefferan, music composition by Paul Castles, and Korean songs by Jongbin Jung. The production stage manager was Melanie J. Lisby. The cast was as follows:

YOO NANHEE . . . . Michelle Krusiec
GUK MINSUNG . . . . Peter Kim
FATHER . . . . Francis Jue
MAN . . . . Joél Pérez
WOMAN . . . . Lulu Fall
HEEJIN . . . . Kendyl Ito
WIFE . . . . Jaygee Macapugay
CHORUS . . . . Dan Domingues, Jamar Williams, Katrina Yaukey

CHARACTERS

YOO NANHEE – North Korean woman, late thirties
GUK MINSUNG – South Korean man, early forties
FATHER – North Korean man, late fifties, Nanhee's father
CHORUS – a chorus of voices, as many as possible, at least five:
MAN – part of chorus / the digital Minsung
WOMAN – part of chorus / the digital Nanhee
HEEJIN – part of chorus / Minsung's daughter
WIFE – part of chorus / Minsung's wife

SETTING

Seoul, South Korea

TIME

Now-ish

PUNCTUATION & FORMATTING NOTES

(–) a cut-off either by self or other
(/) a point where another character might cut in
[words] that are thought but unspoken

Right Alignment
happens when speaker is in another reality

which is different from the speaker with lines in
Left Alignment

Center Alignment
happens when speakers in different realities
speak the same lines simultaneously

For Chorus:
- spoken by one chorus member assigned at director's discretion; all other Chorus lines are spoken in unison
1 is pronounced "one"
0 is pronounced "zero"

#1

FATHER.

Once upon a time there was an angel.

She lived in the heavens with all the other angels.

One day some of them decide to defy the Heavenly Emperor and sneak down to Earth.

Sneak sneak sneak.

They find an earthly river, fling off their heavenly robes and jump in,

they're just chilling, having some earthly fun...and a woodcutter passes by, hears heavenly noises and sneaks up to the river sneak sneak sneak! What does he see? Naked angels. He is so surprised, backs up, and slips on a pile of heavenly robes. Woah. They are so beautiful and so strange he cannot help but take one. Then he creeps off. Creep creep creep.

Sun sets, the angels are exhausted, "Arh! I'm exhausted," they say, "Yeah yeah let's get outta here, let's go grab a heavenly beverage," they dry up and get ready to fly back home except this one angel; "Where are my clothes!" she exclaims, because they can't fly back without their clothes, it's like their wings? Her angel friends feel so bad, but what can they do? So they say sorry and goodbye. And the lonely angel stays in the river, cold, hungry and very angry.

Next day, the woodcutter returns to find the angel girl, still cold, hungry and very angry. He says, "Please angel come to my home. I make some really good seaweed soup." Angel girl thinks, food. Mmmmm FOOD. And all of her cold and anger? It is gone for a time.

They have the yummy soup, she gets earthly clothes, they fall in love get married have lots of angel-human babies, babies grow up and go off to college, and they are growing old together.

Then one day, the once-angel finds her heavenly robes hidden under the floorboards of her house. Panicked and scared, Woodcutter cuts in, "No no I can explain." And he does, and he cries, and she cries, and they share a renewed love that had gotten stale after years of domestic stasis. And then she puts on the robes. Woodcutter is so surprised he says, "But what about our family? Our love? You are my wife!" Angel girl says, "Fuck you. I can fly." And then she disappears into the heavens never to return.

If you have to choose between family and flying, I hope you would choose the flying.

And don't tell Mommy I said that.

Also don't tell Mommy I said fuck you.

Okay. Time for bed. Everyone go to sleep now.

#2

CHORUS.

• Please restart your system to install important updates.

Vooooooooooooong Bum!*

• LOVE THIS!
• Like.
• LOVE THIS!
• Like.
• This kitten.
• This puppy!

THIS.

• Breaking News! Presidential summit at the DMZ cancelled due to –
• POP-UP: Win a free trip to the paradise of your dreams –
• Ding! From calendar. Traffic is slower than usual leave now for / meeting with –
• POP-UP: You know you deserve this special –
• Close. Look up: traffic in Seoul, search –
• 010/01 01 01 001 01 – • SEARCHING, SEARCHING, SEARCHING, SEARCHING
• There are about 203,000 results for traffic in Seoul –
• Ding Dong! Fine dust alert, / do not leave your –
• Delete –
• 1011/00101 – • DELETING
• Deleted.
• Look up: cheap flights to Connecticut, search –
• 010/01 01 – • SEARCHING, SEARCHING
• There are about / 45,000 results –
• Breaking News! Presidential summit still happening according to –
• Delete –
• 1011 / 00101 –
• Deleting –
• What's on Your Mind?
• What's on Your Mind?
• What's on Your –

[MUSIC NO. 01 "INTERNET CHORUS I"]

• 1011 –
• WHAT'S ON YOUR

	CHORUS 1.		CHORUS 2.
	10111	**WOMAN.**	• What's on your mind?
MAN.	001010	SCROLL.	What's on your mind?
SCROLL.	011001		
SCROLL.	11101		

*The sound of a computer rebooting.

	00111		• Ding! From calendar. Traffic is slower than usual. Leave now for meeting with / –
	001001		
	11001	DELETE.	101100101
			• POP-UP: Breaking News! Missile tests resume from the North.
	• What's on your / mind?	GO TO LINK.	
	What's on your mind?		101100
SCROLL.	What's on your mind?		10110 –
ESCAPE.		ESCAPE.	
			• Ding! From calendar. Traffic is slower than –
	• POP-UP: Breaking / –		
DELETE		DELETE.	
LOOK UP: CHICKEN AND BEER DELIVERY,	101100101		101100101
SEARCH.			
	01 001	DELETE.	• Ding! From calendar –
SEARCH.			101100
SEARCH.	• LOADING.	DELETE.	10 Ding!
SEARCH.	• LOADING.		10 Ding!
		DELETE.	
REFRESH.	01001	DELETE.	10 Ding!
SEARCH.		DELETE.	Dingdingdingding.
SEARCH.		DELETE.	

CHORUS.
No response.

MAN.
Search.

WOMAN.
Escape.

CHORUS.
No response.

MAN & WOMAN.
Close.

CHORUS.
• System not responding.

MAN & WOMAN.
Reboot.

CHORUS.
Vooooooooooooong Bum!
• Katok Katok!

WOMAN.
You have one new Talk from Song Ji Ah.

CHORUS.
• Nanhee, it's Ji Ah. Here's the number for my broker. He goes by Mister Lee. Not cheap but worth it.

MAN.
Poke Heejin Cook. You have successfully poked Heejin Cook. Minsung, what's on your mind?

WOMAN.
Nanhee, what's on your mind?

CHORUS.
Brinng Brinng
Brinng Brinng
Brinng Brinng
Brinng.
• The account you're trying to reach is currently unavailable. Leave a message after the Peeeeeeeeeeeeeeeep.

NANHEE.
Mister Lee, hello. This is Yoo Nanhee.
I got your number from my friend Song Ji Ah,
she said you were able to connect her to her family in the North.
I too have family in North Korea, I defected about four years ago.
And I want to smuggle a phone to them as well.
If you can help, please call me at this number.
Again, my name is Yoo Nanhee. Thank you.

CHORUS.
Brinng Peeeeeeeeeeeeeeeep.

MINSUNG.
Hello from Seoul, it's me, Minsung.
I'm alone at the office.
I called our daughter but she is not picking up, so,
I am calling the wife. Hi Wife.
Seven years and I still can't get the time difference right. Sorry.
Anyway. Call me when you can.
I'll be here all night.
Be well.

CHORUS.
• Disconnected.

MAN.
Open email.

CHORUS.
• No new emails.

WOMAN.
Open messages.

CHORUS.
• No new messages.

MAN & WOMAN.
Open Facebook.

CHORUS.
• No new Facebook notifications.

MAN.
Scroll.

WOMAN.
Scroll.

CHORUS.
• Twenty-eight reasons skinny is the new fat.
• Twenty-one images of humanity.
• Epic fails.
• The best no-makeup look with makeup.

WOMAN.
Save.

CHORUS.
• Why *Footloose* was the *Frozen* of the eighties.
• I NEED A HERO I'M HOLDING OUT FOR A –
• Loneliness the true cause of addiction.

MAN.
Escape.

CHORUS.
• More senior citizens living alone in Seoul than ever before.

WOMAN.
Escape

*(**CHORUS** sings a few lines from an upbeat pop song about being lonely.*)*

CHORUS.
• Depressed? Lonely? Sad? Join us at Praise on Wednesdays dot Onnuri Church dot.

MAN & WOMAN.
Escape.

---

*A license to produce *Wild Goose Dreams* does not include a performance license for any third-party or copyrighted music. Licensees should create an original composition or use music in the public domain. For further information, please see Music Use Note on page 3.

CHORUS.

• No new Facebook notifications.

• No new messages.

WOMAN.
Open Tetris.

MAN.
Open Angry Birds.

(Brief non-pre-recorded gaming sounds from **CHORUS.***)*

CHORUS.

• *(KakaoTalk notification.)* Katok! Katok!

WOMAN.
You have one new Talk from Love Genie.

CHORUS.
AH

WOMAN.
Congratulations, Yoo Nanhee!
You've been selected for a one-month free trial membership at Love Genie dot Co dot Kr.
Thousands of elite men are just waiting for your poke of love. Join now!

CHORUS.
AH

MAN.
Welcome back, MrGooseMan! You have no new messages.

WOMAN.
Are you sure you would like to delete this talk?

CHORUS.
1011 00101

WOMAN.
Talk deleted.

MAN.
Scroll.

WOMAN.
Scroll.

CHORUS.

• Ping! Newsletter from Nature. Penguin Factoids. Click / here to unsubscribe.

• POP-UP: Seven reasons why reunification will benefit both / Koreas.

• Breaking News! / Terror!

• What's on your mind?

• What's / on your mind? What's on your –

[MUSIC NO. 02 "INTERNET CHORUS II"]

• 1011 What's on your –

• 1011 What's on your 1011?

• Ding! From / calendar.

• POP-UP: Remember me?

WOMAN.	**MAN.**	**CHORUS 1.**	**CHORUS 2.**
		1011100101	
ESCAPE.	GO TO LINK.		
BROKER MISTER LEE.		10110010110	
	ESCAPE.		
SEARCH.		0100101	
	GO TO FACEBOOK.	0100101	101100101100
	SIGN IN.		
DELETE.		010010101	
			101100101
	MINSUNG YOU HAVE NINE FRIENDS.		
DEFECTOR BROKER LEE.			
SEARCH.	SEARCH: HEEJIN COOK IN FAIRFIELD.		
FOUR MILLION RESULTS.		0100101	
DELETE.		0100101	101100101
	SCROLL.	0100101	10111001010
	SCROLL.		
		0100	01100111101
REFRESH.	SCROLL.	JAVA SCRIPT OPEN POP-UP.	
		101100.	00111001001110
	DELETE REFRESH.		
SMUGGLING PHONES TO THE NORTH SEARCH.	GO.	101100	
ABORT SEARCH.	SEARCH: FLIGHTS.	101100	01
	SEARCH.		

CHORUS.
Brinng Brinng.
Brinng Brinng.
Brinng Brinng.
• Connecting.

MINSUNG.
Heejin? How are you? How is America? How is school? Sad? Why? What? Why are you sad about an A-minus in World History?

NANHEE.
Hello? Father?
It's me. Nanhee. Your daughter.
Can you hear me? Hello?
Yes it's really me. I didn't drown in the river. I am alive, in the south.

MINSUNG.
Don't be sad, it's okay! You are my daughter. You are a genius.

NANHEE.
What? I can't hear you very well.

MINSUNG.
Genius. You don't know that word? In English it is **big head.*** **Big Einstein head.**
Daddy have Einstein head, Daughter have Einstein head, understand?
It is extra? I don't know what –
Ah. Heejin. That is not very respectful of your father.

NANHEE.
Are you crying? Please don't cry Father,
I am very alive and very successful.
I have sent you money through the broker, Mister Lee, who gave you the phone.
Did you get it?

MINSUNG.
A boyfriend.

NANHEE.
What?
I think the connection is very bad, there is a lot of static noise – can you speak louder?
Hello?

MINSUNG.
Heejin, could you slow down please Daddy is not so good at English.
Boyfriend yes? Boyfriend no?

NANHEE.
Oh! Yes of course I have a husband, and children.

MINSUNG.
Heejin, show Daddy **boyfriend photograph.**

NANHEE.
Sons. Two sons. I have two children who are male and I am very happy and very successful.

MINSUNG.
Oh. **Burrito.** I thought you said **boyfriend.**
Well, send a picture when you have one, okay?
Or you could friend me on Facebook? I have applied to be your friend.
Why? I can friend. Daddy will good friend. C'mon. It'll be fun. **Yes?!**

NANHEE.
Yes I am happy. Of course I am happy.
I never thought I would hear your voice ever again, and there you are.
I am sorry, for everything.

MINSUNG.
Already? My daughter is the busiest girl in Fairfield, Connecticut.

---

*Words in bold should be spoken in a heavy Korean accent.

MINSUNG & NANHEE.
Be healthy, okay?

CHORUS.
• Disconnected.

NANHEE.
Hello?
...
Open trash.

CHORUS.
AH

WOMAN.
Congratulations, Yoo Nanhee!
You've been selected for a one-month free trial membership at Love Genie dot Co dot Kr.
Thousands of elite men are just waiting for your poke of love. Join now!

NANHEE.
Join.

MAN.
Minsung, what's on your mind?

MINSUNG.
View friends.

MAN.
You have nine friends.

WOMAN.
Enter username to create your new profile.

MAN.
Guk Minsung sent Heejin Cook a friend request.

NANHEE.
QueenNanhee.

WOMAN.
Is already in use.

MINSUNG.
Refresh browser.

NANHEE.
NanheeIsPretty.

WOMAN.
Is already in use.

MINSUNG.
Add friend.

MAN.
You have already sent a request to Heejin Cook.

NANHEE.
NanheeIsPretty81.

WOMAN.
Is already in use.

MINSUNG.
Go to Love Genie.

CHORUS.
AH

MAN.
Welcome back, MrGooseMan.

NANHEE.
MinersDaughter.

WOMAN.
Is available. Would you like to claim it?

MAN.
You have no new messages.

WOMAN.
Congratulations, MinersDaughter!

CHORUS.
- Welcome!
- To the land of *love* where you will finally meet that person of your dreams.
- Click here to browse your matches.

WOMAN.
We have found twenty-five new matches! Would you like to send a love poke?
Message from MinersDaughter:

NANHEE.
Hello you look very nice I love your eyes.
Would you like to create grandsons for my father just kidding.
Say hello back if you like stupid jokes such as above!

WOMAN.
Sent to PrettyBoy123, Select All Copy Paste.
Hello you look very nice I love your eyes.
Would you like to blahdiblahdiblah such as above!
Sent to JustANormalDudeISwear, Copy Paste.
Hello you look very etc.
Sent to Iamthefifthbeatle Copy Paste.
Hello you etc., Sent to DumpsterFireZZZ. Sent to –
Retrieve message to DumpsterFireZZZ.
Sent to / MrGooseMan.

MAN.
MrGooseMan! You have one new message. Would you like to reply to MinersDaughter?
Hello back. You look very nice too. Do you like karaoke?
Sent to –

MAN & WOMAN.
MinersDaughter.

WOMAN.
You have one new message. Would you like to reply to –
I've never been to karaoke.
Send.

MAN.
You've never been to karaoke never ever? That's crazy! Smiling Crying Face.
Send.

WOMAN.
Why?
Send.

MAN.
I don't know anyone who's never been to karaoke before! Surprised Face with Hands on Cheeks.
Send.

WOMAN.
I'm from North Korea. Defector.
Send.

MAN.
Oh wow.
Send.

WOMAN.
Is that weird? Send.

MAN.
No! I love North Korea I've always wanted to go to – Delete.
How are you liking capitalism? Is it very different than – Delete.
What the hell am I supposed to say to that of course it's weird delete delete.

WOMAN.
?
Send.

MAN.
I'm married.
Send.

WOMAN.
...?
Send.
Is that a joke? Send.
Sometimes I don't get South Korean jokes. Send.

MAN.
Yes. It's a joke, a South Korean joke, you wouldn't understand because –
Delete delete delete.
No. Not a joke.
Send.

WOMAN.
I guess no grandsons for my father. Send.

MAN.
Not from me, as far as – Delete.
LOL. Send.

WOMAN.
Why are you on this website? Send.

MAN & MINSUNG.
I'm lonely.

WOMAN & NANHEE.
Oh.

NANHEE.
That makes me sad.

MINSUNG.
Me too. Why are You on this website?

NANHEE.
I got a free trial in my inbox.
But mostly because I am lonely too.

MINSUNG.
So. Karaoke? Maybe?

NANHEE.
Probably not a good –
Delete.

WOMAN.
As friends? Smiley face.
Send.

MAN.
Of course! Thumbs up thumbs up smiley face.
Send.

*(**CHORUS** erupts into individual renditions of Noraebang singing [Korean karaoke].*)*

---

*A license to produce *Wild Goose Dreams* does not include a performance license for any third-party or copyrighted music. Licensees should create an original composition or use music in the public domain. For further information, please see Music Use Note on page 3.

#3

*(**MINSUNG** and **NANHEE** are in a bed. **FATHER** sits somewhere nearby.)*

MINSUNG.
I am a responsible man. I will take care of you.

NANHEE.
Thank you.

MINSUNG.
And the baby. If there is a baby.

(He plays with his phone.)

CHORUS.
- No new emails.
- No new messages.
- No new Facebook notifications.

MINSUNG.
But I could never get a divorce that would be bad for us –

NANHEE.
Mhm.

MINSUNG.
Because this is an affair.

CHORUS.
- Search: Husband affair asset division.
- Askkorealaw dot com Q&A.
- Q. My dirty husband is sexing with our daughter's tutor. Will I get rich if I divorce him or should I make him suffer?
- A. Make him suffer.

MINSUNG.
Although, my wife and daughter have been in America for seven years, I don't think they'd know if I lit myself on fire, how will they know that I'm having an affair? They call us the goose fathers, I could look that up for you.

CHORUS.
- Search: Goose father origin.
- Wikipedia Korea.

MINSUNG.
Aha.

CHORUS.
- The goose father is a Korean man who works in Korea while his wife and children stay in an English-speaking country for the sake of the children's education. / The term is –

MINSUNG.
The term is inspired by the fact that geese migrate, just as the goose dad must travel a great distance to see his family.

NANHEE.
That's nice.

MINSUNG.
I'm just babbling on like the Energizer Bunny blablablablablah. Sorry.

Ah. That is probably not what you want to hear. I know women do not like to hear it when a man apologizes. Especially after. Maybe before is okay. During is terrible. Or is it sexy? Is it sexy to apologize during sex in North Korea?

Nanhee, is it sexy to apologize during sex in North Korea?

NANHEE.
It depends on the North Korean you are apologizing to.

MINSUNG.
Oh. Are you angry with me?

NANHEE.
No.

MINSUNG.
You look angry. Or sad. Or far away. Like you are unsatisfied with me.

Was it not good? Did you not like the sex we had?

NANHEE.
My father is here.

MINSUNG.
Hm?!

NANHEE.
My father. He is here.

MINSUNG.
Your father? Where?

NANHEE.
There. He appeared when you first entered.

MINSUNG.
When I entered?

NANHEE.
Me.

MINSUNG.
Oh. Is that a joke? A North Korean joke?

NANHEE.
No.

MINSUNG.
Did it help your sex to see him?

NANHEE.
No.

MINSUNG.
Have you dealt with your guilt?

NANHEE.
Excuse me?

MINSUNG.
I looked up North Korean defectors. On YouTube? I was preparing for our date.

*(**FATHER** grunts, like he is annoyed.)*

(He leaves to the bathroom.)

*(**NANHEE** follows him.)*

Many people were having problems of guilt. Maybe government brainwashing has made you feel guilty about leaving your Fatherland – I'm sorry that was a stupid thing to say.

(The bathroom door is locked.)

NANHEE.
It's locked.

MINSUNG.
Maybe I locked it by mistake. I used it after we – Did you need to go?

(Sound of pee hitting the water in the toilet bowl.)

NANHEE.
Oh!

MINSUNG.
What?

NANHEE.
He's peeing.

MINSUNG.
Should I leave?

NANHEE.
This is your place.

MINSUNG.
It's not.

NANHEE.
Did we drunkenly walk into somebody else's place?

MINSUNG.
No, we drunkenly walked into a motel.

NANHEE.
You said this was your place.

MINSUNG.
I think I drunkenly lied.

NANHEE.
Why?

MINSUNG.
I don't know. I wanted to impress you.

(Peeing stops for a bit.)

NANHEE.
Oh. That is nice.
Is that how South Korean men impress women, take them to a motel?

MINSUNG.
If they live in a *koshiwon*, motels seem the better option.

(Flushing sound. Other noisy sounds from the bathroom continue.)

A *koshiwon* is a small room for students who are preparing for exams. The bed folds out from the wall and the showerhead hangs directly over the toilet bowl.

NANHEE.
I know what a *koshiwon* is. Are you preparing for exams?

MINSUNG.
No, it is the most cheap and convenient housing. I have a very good salary, but I am sending it all to my family in another country.

NANHEE.
Me too. Only, I can't be sure that they actually get what I send.

(Gunshot from bathroom mid-bathroom sounds.)

*(**NANHEE** makes a sound of sharp surprise and fear.)*

MINSUNG.
What? What's wrong?

*(**NANHEE** opens the bathroom door; it's no longer locked. She runs in.)*

Are you angry with me? I can still take care of you, I have enough for that.
But. I cannot get a divorce. That is my limit. My only limit. No divorce.

*(**NANHEE** returns.)*

*(**FATHER** is back in the room somewhere. Maybe on the bed.)*

FATHER.
He is not very good-looking for a South Korean Man.

MINSUNG.
I'm sorry but it is for my daughter, I cannot free myself from my daughter.

FATHER.
That's a lot of baggage to take on for a not-good-looking South Korean Man.

MINSUNG.
You look worried.

FATHER.
You do. Is it me or is it him.

NANHEE.
I want to leave.

MINSUNG.
Now?

NANHEE.
Where is my bra.

MINSUNG.
Did I say something wrong?

NANHEE.
I can't find my bra.

MINSUNG.
Is it because of the divorce? The no divorce rule?

FATHER.
I think I saw him hide it.

NANHEE.
Did you hide my bra?

MINSUNG.
What? Hide? I didn't hide –

NANHEE.
Keep it.

FATHER.
Maybe he hid it under the floorboards so you can't fly away?
Like the angel and the woodcutter!

NANHEE.
I don't need my bra to fly away.

MINSUNG.
Okay?

FATHER.
I know you don't sweetie, it was a metaphor.

MINSUNG.
Hey. Nanhee. What is going on.

NANHEE.
I spoke with my father the other day.

FATHER.
First time in four years.

MINSUNG.
I thought your family was still on the other side.

FATHER.
We are.

NANHEE.
They are. We smuggled a phone.

FATHER.
She did.

MINSUNG.
A phone? You can do that?

NANHEE.
I guess so.

FATHER.
And I wept with joy!
Through tears I said,
I can't believe you are alive are you married do you have children and are they male!

NANHEE.
But I, um, lied about having sons.

MINSUNG.
...Sons?

NANHEE.
He was crying, I was feeling, feelings, and I wanted him to know I was okay. So I said I have two sons and a husband and then looked for potential husband and two sons on the internet.

MINSUNG.
Oh.

FATHER.
But then she found you.

MINSUNG.
So you think he appeared to say no don't do that –

FATHER.
I didn't say anything like that.

MINSUNG.
Like your conscience?

FATHER.
I just watched and then said he was a not-good-looking man with a lot of baggage.

MINSUNG.
He came to say, it's okay I don't need you to find babies on the internet?

FATHER.
Don't listen to him I want the babies.

NANHEE.
Shut up! Just everyone, sht.

MINSUNG & FATHER.
Oh. Sorry.

NANHEE.
I'm, leaving.

MINSUNG.
Okay let's go.

FATHER.
About time.

NANHEE.
No! You, stay.

MINSUNG.
This really is not my apartment.

FATHER.
I don't want to stay. I don't know that guy.

MINSUNG.
Um wait Nanhee.

NANHEE.
What?

MINSUNG.
Just, here's my card, if you need anything at all.

NANHEE.
Keep the card. Keep the bra. Keep everything. Thank you. Thank you for the sex. Goodbye.

(She's gone.)

MINSUNG.
Oh.

(His phone rings.)

CHORUS.
Brinng Brinng
Brinng Brinng
Brinng Brinng

*(***MINSUNG** *checks caller ID.)*

Brinng Brinng
Brinng Brinng
Brinng.

MINSUNG.
Hello Wife.
Oh thank you. Yes I did something special for my birthday.
Oh. That's okay. We're too old for birthday presents, anyway.
Yes. The salary is slim this month.
No I am not drinking away the money. The company withheld –
Oh. I didn't know it was a joke. Haha.
Already? Okay. Thanks for calling. Be well. I miss –

CHORUS.
• Disconnected

MINSUNG.
You.

MAN.
Compose new email
To: Wife.

MINSUNG.
Dear Wifey,
For my birthday I wish for you to miss me.
I wish to be more than an ATM machine that needs to be called at times such as birthdays. Haha.
I wish for you to flirt with me, cry for me, send me care packages with thick socks and those terrible American snacks, like you used to do.
I wish I knew how you taste now.
I wish I knew when you are joking or not.

I wish you were more real for me.
I wish I were more real for you.

MAN.
Are you sure you'd like to close the browser?
Save or Discard draft?

MINSUNG.
Discard.

(He crawls back into bed with a certain sadness.)

(And comes back up with a bra.)

(Smells it.)

(It's nice.)

#4

CHORUS.

• MinersDaughter, it's been a whole week since your very first Genie date! Tell us all about it and receive another free month of membership.

• Katok! Katok!

• Nanhee, it's Ji Ah. How did it work out with the broker Mister Lee?

• Dear Miss Yoo, Office is out of coffee and orange juice. Would you take care of that ASAP?

FATHER.
It's very interesting, your life.

NANHEE.
Thank you.

FATHER.
Is that your whole job? Stocking beverages for the office workers of the South Korean Government?

NANHEE.
Of course not. I'm just, in the process of climbing the social ladder of capitalism.

FATHER.
Very impressive.

NANHEE.
Thank you.
Are you saying that because my mind wants you to say that
or because you are really saying that?
Because you aren't really my father, just the father that has been created by my mind, right?
Am I going crazy?

FATHER.
That's okay sweetie. Sometimes a broken mind is the only way to find comfort.
Come on. Let's go find some coffee and orange juice.

NANHEE.
We do it on the internet.

HEEJIN.
Heejin Cook accepted your friend request. Write on Heejin's wall.

MAN.
Hello Daughter! I am so happy we are friends! Do you have a boyfriend yet?

HEEJIN.
Message from Heejin Cook:
Hiya Pops! FYI no stuff on the wall, just pm me if u wanna chat, k?

MAN.
What is pm?

HEEJIN.
OMG you are so extra, just write wot u wanna say in the space below this msg.

MAN.
MSG? Like the ingredient?

HEEJIN.
LMAO no sorry, I meant message. But you did it right you sent that last one as a msg.

MAN.
Smiley face with bulging hearts for eyes thumbs up thumbs up.

HEEJIN.
Smiley face with bulging hearts for eyes thumbs up thumbs up Imma go delete ur wallposts, k?

FATHER.
Let's go out tonight! Call all your friends! I want to meet them.

NANHEE.
How?

FATHER.
A one-way meeting. Aren't you curious what I think of your rich flashy South Korean friends?

NANHEE.
I don't have any.

FATHER.
Really?

NANHEE.
What?

FATHER.
It's just so unlike you, to have no friends.

CHORUS.
AH

WOMAN.
MrGooseMan has logged in.

FATHER.
Well, you have that guy.

NANHEE.
I do have that guy.

MAN.
Message from MrGooseMan: Hello lady!

WOMAN.
Hi.

MAN.
We should go out again. I have something that belongs to you. Smiley devil face.

FATHER.
He kept your bra. Winner.

NANHEE.
Don't be so judge-y.

I'm over thirty and haven't had plastic surgery. I'm surprised he's still talking to me two weeks after sex.

MAN.
Wanna go Karaoke again?

WOMAN.
It was very loud. Monkey with hands over ears.

MAN.
Hahahah. Laughing with tears.
Do you like sushi? There's a delicious sushi place in my neighborhood.

FATHER.
Sushi!

WOMAN.
I love sushi.

FATHER.
I love tuna sashimi.

WOMAN.
Especially tuna sashimi.

FATHER.
I haven't had tuna sashimi since I was demoted and sent to the mines after your outburst at school about why the motherland isn't doing anything to get the buses running again.

MAN.
Sashimi is their specialty! So wanna go?

FATHER.
I say yes to sashimi.

NANHEE.
You are not coming.

MAN.
I dropped you a pin on maps.

FATHER.
Yes I am.

MAN.
Did you get it?

NANHEE.
No you are not. This is a date! For Two people.

FATHER.
So? I have already seen you in bed with this guy. Let me watch you eat sashimi!

MAN.
What do you think?

WOMAN.
Sorry. Something came up. Raincheck?

CHORUS.

• First snow of the year!

• It is only October our earth is dying. WAKE UP / PEOPLE!

• MinersDaughter, your one-month free trial membership has expired. Would you like to renew your subscription?

WOMAN.

Renew subscription.

CHORUS.

• Dear Miss Yoo, Office is out of coffee and orange juice again, would you take care of that ASAP?

WOMAN.

Reply to all.

CHORUS.

• *(KakaoTalk notification.)* Katok! Katok!

• Hey Nanhee, it's Ji Ah. Have you heard from Mister Lee at all?

FATHER.

He's a fraud.

NANHEE.

What?

WOMAN.

Dear team.

FATHER.

Mister Lee. He's a fraud.

WOMAN.

Thank you for your fraud.

NANHEE.

Fuck.

WOMAN.

Delete delete.

Thank you for bringing this to my attention. I will restock ASAP.

CHORUS.

• Heejin Cook has been tagged in Jimmy Kai's album.

• Jimmy Kai commented: Taco Tuesdays with the fabulous Cook Ladies. You have not lived till you've had Heejin's Kimchi Guacamole! Bulging hearts for eyes.

HEEJIN.

Heejin Cook likes this.

MAN.

You…

MINSUNG.

Like this.

MAN.

Poke Heejin Cook.

NANHEE.
Mister Lee is a good man. He was recommended by a fellow defector.

CHORUS.
• *(KakaoTalk notification.)* Katok! Katok!
• Hey Nanhee, it's Ji Ah. Don't know if you heard but Lee went AWOL. Some say he ran a scam, some say he got caught and gave info on all the families he delivered to. Everyone is freaking out. Let me know if you hear anything, k? Yours, Ji Ah.

(Gunshot.)

FATHER.
Uh-oh.

NANHEE.
Mister Lee is a good man.

MAN.
MinersDaughter where did you go?

WOMAN.
MinersDaughter is unavailable to chat.

CHORUS.
• Miss Yoo, were you unable to find coffee and orange juice? Some colleagues are complaining.

FATHER.
Do you think Mister Lee betrayed you?

NANHEE.
No.

MAN.
I went on another Genie date. I was thinking about you all night. Hope you are well.

FATHER.
I think Mister Lee betrayed you.

NANHEE.
He did not look like that kind of man.

FATHER.
You don't look like that kind of daughter but look how you betrayed me.

NANHEE.
You would never say that. My father would never say that.

FATHER.
Four years is a long time. People change.
You've changed.

MAN.
Where did you go?

CHORUS.
• Dear Miss Yoo, Surely it cannot be that hard to –

[MUSIC NO. 03 "INTERNET CHORUS III"]

WOMAN.
DELETE.

CHORUS.
• 10/ 11 00101

MAN.
You there? Hello? / Monkey with hands over eyes.

CHORUS.
• 010 / 01 01 0
• Dear Miss Yoo, Please respond immediate/ly to –

WOMAN.
DELETE.

CHORUS.
• 10 / 11 00101
• What's on your –
• 10111 001010 011001 11101...*

FATHER.
I wouldn't recognize you. You barely recognized me.

NANHEE.
Shut up.

CHORUS.
• What's on your mind what's on your mind?

FATHER.
You don't know if that guy on the phone was actually me, do you?

NANHEE.
I said shut up!

WOMAN.
Shut down.

CHORUS.
• Are you sure you want to shut down your computer now?

MAN.
MinersDaughter, come back.

WOMAN.
Shut down.

(A quiet moment, soon interrupted by:)

CHORUS.
• Dear Miss Yoo. I am sorry to hear you have been feeling unwell. However, our office has zero tolerance for unnotified sick leave. Please be ready to attend evaluation committee with explanation about the past two days. Click here for format of apology letter.
PEEEEEEEEEEEP.

NANHEE.
Mister Lee.

---

*Continue under scene until **WOMAN**'s second "Shut down."

MINSUNG.
Hello Wife.

MINSUNG & NANHEE.
I don't know how to say this.

MINSUNG.
I am not a jealous man you know this.

NANHEE.
But there are rumors concerning your honesty.

MINSUNG.
Heejin is my friend, on Facebook I mean –
And there is all over her wall pictures of you and the –
Jimmy Kai –

NANHEE.
The other defectors.
They have had phone calls with their families.
But later on they turned out to be fake families.

MINSUNG.
He is a divorced man, I saw, because I went on his Facebook, you are his friend on Facebook.
I did not even know you were on Facebook.

MINSUNG & NANHEE.
And I need to know.

NANHEE.
Did you find a fake father for me?

MINSUNG.
Do you just want to be my wife for my salary?

NANHEE.
You have not picked up the phone for several weeks.
And my fake father's number is not in service.
And I have sent you so much money you fucking son of a dicksquash.

MINSUNG.
Have I wasted my salary? Are you no longer my wife?

NANHEE.
I am sorry I cursed.

MINSUNG.
I am sorry if I am overreacting.

MINSUNG & NANHEE.
Just please, tell the truth.

MINSUNG.
I feel old and useless. Please call me.

NANHEE.
Please call.

CHORUS.

- Disconnected.
- *(KakaoTalk notification.)* Katok! Katok! From Unknown.
- Miss Yoo, this is Lee. Do not attempt further contact. Your family's lives are at stake.

WOMAN.
Reply to Unknown:

NANHEE.
My family's lives? Why? What happened?

WOMAN.
Send.

CHORUS.

- Message cannot be sent.

WOMAN.
Send.

CHORUS.

- Message cannot be sent.

FATHER.
Told you so.

(Gunshot.)

HEEJIN.
Message from Heejin Cook: WTF OMG Dad untag me from that pic WTHIWWY?!?!

MINSUNG.
Hi!

HEEJIN.
Delete! Plz! Idk wot u doin Imma unfriend u if u do shit lyk dis 2 me.

MINSUNG.
Huh?

HEEJIN.
Picture! Photo! Photograph of me butt naked with a banana in my face!

MINSUNG.
Yes! You are three years old! I am happy you like it.

MAN.
Smiley face with bulging hearts for eyes.

HEEJIN.
FML yr killin me. Sorry Dad I'm blockin u.

MINSUNG.
Heejin I don't understand what you are writing. Everything is okay?

CHORUS.

- Sorry, this page isn't available.
- The link you followed may be broken, or the page may have been removed.

MAN.
Compose new email.

MINSUNG.
Dear Daughter, I don't know what happened but I can't find you anymore.
Daddy will fix and everything will be okay. I love you. From Dad.

CHORUS.
- Mail Delivery Subsystem MAILER DAEMON: the following address had permanent fatal errors.

MINSUNG.
Delete.

(Gunshot.)

NANHEE.
Are you dead? Is that why you are here? Did they kill you?

FATHER.
Didn't know you cared.

NANHEE.
That's not fair.

FATHER.
You left us to cross the river. You knew what that meant for us.

NANHEE.
You said choose flying.
If I had to choose between family and flying, choose flying, you said.

FATHER.
As in go to Pyongyang, have an awesome job, not sneak away into the river like a common traitor.

CHORUS.
- JINGLE BELLS JINGLE BELLS
- Holiday special movie of the past, watch *Home Alone Two* with your family / on channel –
- Ten best end of year party venues in Seoul.

MAN.
Message from MrGooseMan: Merry Christmas. Are you doing something special?

FATHER.
Look, if you are happy in your paradise, that's one thing.

NANHEE.
I am very happy.

FATHER.
When you are not talking to fake fathers on the phone you are talking to one in your head. This is the happy that's worth the safety of your whole family?

NANHEE.
What am I supposed to do? Go back?
I'm supposed to go back to North Korea?

*(**FATHER** kisses his daughter on her forehead, leaves.)*

CHORUS.
Five Four Three Two One.

(**CHORUS** *celebrates the New Year with "Auld Lang Syne."*)

MAN.
Message from MrGooseMan: Happy New Year.
I watched the sunrise from Walnut Beach, Connecticut. Did you watch the sunrise?
Message from MrGooseMan: I cleaned my tiny room today!
It smells like floor wax. I love the smell of floor wax. Do you?
Message from MrGooseMan –

MINSUNG.
I wrote a song. I think it's about you.

MAN.
Smiley face.

MINSUNG.
Well I know it's about you. I know it's about you because I wrote it for you.

MAN.
Smiley face!

MINSUNG.
It's not terrible. I used to make music before I made phones for Samsung.
I used to be in a band. I played the bass. That's how I stole my wife's heart.

MAN.
Wink smiley face.
Recall previous message.
I used to have a band. I was the lead. I wrote lots of music.
That's how I got all the girls. Wink smiley face.

MINSUNG.
But it's pretty stupid. I'm pretty stupid. I can't stop thinking about you.

MAN.
Sad face.
Recall previous message.
I know it was a one-night stand but I want more one-night stands with you.

MINSUNG.
Where did you go. Where did you go. Where did you go. I wish you were more real for me.

CHORUS.
AH

WOMAN.
MinersDaughter has logged in.

MAN & MINSUNG.
Recall all unread messages!

WOMAN.
Failed.

MAN & MINSUNG.
Recall all unread messages!

WOMAN.
Failed.

MAN & MINSUNG.
Recall all unread –

WOMAN.
Recipient has read all messages.

MAN.
Logout.

WOMAN.
Message from MinersDaughter: Wow it's like you wrote a whole novel.

MAN.
MrGooseMan is no longer available to chat.

WOMAN.
Message from MinersDaughter –

NANHEE.
What's the song? Can I hear it?

#5

[MUSIC NO. 04 "I AM REAL"]

MINSUNG.

진짜라짜짜 진짜라니까 나
가짜라짜짜라니 맘이 아파와
진짜 숨소리
진짜 마음이
진짜라짜짜보라니까 진짜야

왜 날 의심해
왜 날 무시해
왜 날 잊으려해
하룻밤의 우리 소중한 추억
왜 날 싫어해
다 날 싫어해
내가 잘할게
하룻밤만 더 내게
기회를 줘

진짜라짜짜 진짜라니까 나
가짜라짜짜라니 눈물만 나와
진짜 심장이
진짜 나대니
진짜라짜짜보라니까 진짜야

#6

NANHEE.
I like it.

MINSUNG.
It's stupid.

NANHEE.
Yes.

MINSUNG.
Oh.

NANHEE.
Stupid, in a funny way. It's a form of South Korean comedy. No?

MINSUNG.
I wasn't intending the song for comedy.

NANHEE.
Oh.

(**MINSUNG** *plays with his phone.)*

CHORUS.
- No new emails.
- No new messages.
- No new Facebook notifications.
- Sports Chosun Today: Something champion football golf blah blah.

MINSUNG.
What made you change your mind?

NANHEE.
About what?

MINSUNG.
You left the website, I left messages but you never checked them. Then you changed your mind.

NANHEE.
Yes. I did.

MINSUNG.
I was caught off guard. All those things I wrote, I was just writing, like poking on Facebook.
Do you do Facebook? They have things called poking.
It serves no purpose but to say hello I'm here.
I used to poke my daughter several times a day, before she blocked me.
Anyway.
So I was writing like I was poking, with no real purpose behind my words.
So I was worried, when you said to meet up, even after you read my embarrassing poke-type messages, because most times when a girl wants to meet up after a very long time,
it is because she has a baby.

NANHEE.
I don't.

MINSUNG.
Oh. Good.

*(**NANHEE** begins to take off his pants. He is taken by surprise.)*

Woh!

NANHEE.
Oh.

MINSUNG.
What are you doing?!

NANHEE.
This is not why you invited me here? That's why you wrote the song?

MINSUNG.
I'm, sure, but –

NANHEE.
You don't want to?

MINSUNG.
No no no of course I do –

NANHEE.
I want to have sex.

MINSUNG.
Yes.

NANHEE.
Do you want to have sex?

MINSUNG.
Yes.

NANHEE.
Okay so.

(She yanks his pants off.)

MINSUNG.
Aahraaha!

ANHEE
What?

MINSUNG.
You, my pants –

*(**NANHEE** looks at his penis.)*

NANHEE.
It's not –

MINSUNG.
No!

NANHEE.
That's okay. I will help.

(She touches, fondles, tries.)

Maybe should we turn off the lights?

*(**MINSUNG** claps.)*

(Lights off.)

That's cool.

MINSUNG.
High efficiency.

NANHEE.
May that be true of your penis.

CHORUS.
Tick tock tick tock tock tick tock.

MINSUNG.
Maybe if I, can I touch your, here?

NANHEE.
Okay but you cannot steal this bra it's new.

MINSUNG.
I didn't steal your –
Never mind.

CHORUS.
Tick tock tick tock tock tick tock.

NANHEE.
You sure you don't have any medication to help the –

MINSUNG.
No.

NANHEE.
I wouldn't judge if you did.

MINSUNG.
Great.

CHORUS.
Tick tock tick tock tock tick / tock.

NANHEE.
Wait, muscle spasm, let me switch sides.

MINSUNG.
No more please stop.

(Clap. Lights on.)

NANHEE.
How old are you again?

MINSUNG.
It's got nothing to do with oldness, I'm fine like that in terms of oldness.

NANHEE.
Are you not aroused by me?

MINSUNG.
It's because you are coming on so fast.

NANHEE.
Am I not attractive to you?

MINSUNG.
I need to lead.

NANHEE.
Do you think I am ugly?

MINSUNG.
I will look that up for you, about sexual leaderships.

CHORUS.
- Search: / Sexual leader.

NANHEE.
Is it because I did not have any plastic surgery?

MINSUNG.
What?

NANHEE.
Is it because I am North Korean? I am not sexual to you because I am North Korean?

MINSUNG.
Of course / [not] –

NANHEE.
Why did you write all those things?
Like a diary, you just wrote to some imaginary perfect woman
but now that you see me you don't want any more?
I am used goods for you now? Your one-time North Korean taste?
Am I one-time usage, like the disposable contact lenses in the little plastic pods?

CHORUS.
- Leadership in physical relationships will vary depending on –

MINSUNG.
You see here –

NANHEE.
Even disposable contact lenses are used two or three times before it is discarded.

(She takes his phone and chucks it into the toilet bowl.)

MINSUNG.
Hey!

NANHEE.
Even disposable contact lenses! Do you think I'm less than disposable contact lenses?!

(She cries.)

MINSUNG.
Oh.

(He doesn't know what to do.)

(He finds a napkin, it's kind of used.)

(He hands it to her anyway.)

(He wants to rescue his phone but then decides it is inappropriate to rescue one's phone when one's lady is crying. He pats her on the shoulder. It's awkward.)

It is not because you are like disposable contact lenses.

I think you are very attractive. I did not know you did not have any plastic surgery.

I wrote you a song. You don't write songs for people who you think are like disposable contact lenses. It takes a lot of time and commitment to write a song.

(He desperately wants to play with his phone.)

NANHEE.
My father is gone.

MINSUNG.
Oh! I'm so sorry.

NANHEE.
No, gone from my mind. My mind is no longer broken.
I want it to be broken again. I thought sex with you might break my mind again.

MINSUNG.
That is very high expectation for second time.

NANHEE.
I'm sorry. I'm sorry I threw your phone in the toilet.

MINSUNG.
That's okay. It's, waterproof.
Why do you want to break your mind?

NANHEE.
I got used to having dinner with someone who knows me.

MINSUNG.
Are you lonely?

NANHEE.
Only recently. After my father appeared and then disappeared.

MINSUNG.
How did you make him disappear?

NANHEE.
I didn't. He said I was a traitor and I got angry and asked what do you want, do you want me to come back to North Korea? And as soon as I said that, he was gone. No goodbye, just gone.
Now I am lonely.

MINSUNG.
Fathers don't usually think their daughters are traitors.

NANHEE.
The one in my head did.

MINSUNG.
Maybe the one in your head wasn't your real father?

NANHEE.
He still left an empty space, either way. And now I am the crazy lady who pulls down the pants of married men for the appearance of her father.

MINSUNG.
I am sorry. Are you crying?

NANHEE.
No. Maybe a little bit on the inside.

MINSUNG.
What was it like back there?

NANHEE.
North Korea?

MINSUNG.
Your home.

NANHEE.
Pretty big, for the village. A square house. Simple. We didn't have beds.

MINSUNG.
No beds? We can do that.

(He folds the bed back into the wall.)

No beds. What else?

NANHEE.
My mom would always give everyone hot water before sleep.

*(***MINSUNG*** puts the kettle on.)*

MINSUNG.
Okay.

NANHEE.
And the nights were so dark. We didn't have electricity so night would be so dark.

*(***MINSUNG*** claps. Dark.)*

MINSUNG.
What else.

NANHEE.
You could hear crows sometimes,

MINSUNG.
Kakkaw Kakkaw.

NANHEE.
No more like, *[better crow sound]*.

MINSUNG.
Hey that's pretty good.

NANHEE.
Thanks. And when everyone was asleep I would sneak out.

MINSUNG.
Sneak out?!

NANHEE.
There was a boy.

MINSUNG.
Ha!

NANHEE.
North Korean teenagers know how to fall in love too.

MINSUNG.
And you would sneak out to meet him.

NANHEE.
In the dark.

MINSUNG.
What did you talk about in the dark.

NANHEE.
Dreams.

MINSUNG.
About leaving?

NANHEE.
No. You do not talk about such plans to anybody. Not family, not lovers. You never know who will report you. No we talked about real dreams. What we dreamt the night before.

MINSUNG.
What kind of dreams.

NANHEE.
I dreamt a lot about flying. One time I had a dream that my father gave me a pair of wings. He said Go! Fly! and I could not fly at all, and it turns out the wings were taken from a penguin. I said, what the fuck don't you know penguins cannot fly. Then he got upset, turned into a penguin and said I want my wings back and I said no! They're mine now! And ran away to Alaska. I guess that dream came true a little.

MINSUNG.
You went to Alaska?

NANHEE.
No. But it feels like that sometimes. Cold. Foreign.

MINSUNG.
You know, fathers usually don't want their wings back. If my daughter had that dream I would want someone to tell her, hey dummy, fathers never ever want their wings back. Party it up in Alaska.

NANHEE.
What about you? Tell me one of your dreams.

MINSUNG.
I don't have dreams.

NANHEE.
Make one up.

MINSUNG.
My penis is awake and wants to make you happy.

NANHEE.
Ha, that is your dream?

MINSUNG.
No it is the truth. See?

NANHEE.
Strange. It helped to tell you about my ex-boyfriend.

MINSUNG.
Nothing like that. No, I think when you cried.
It is shameful but my penis is interested in devastated women.

NANHEE.
I am not a –

MINSUNG.
Let us not challenge the fragile penis.

NANHEE.
Of course not.

[MUSIC NO. 05 "SEX MUSIC"]

(A beautiful, harmonious song, reminiscent of the Love Genie jingle.)

MAN & WOMAN.
LA LA
LA LA LA LA LA LA LA LA

(Oh wait.)

*(**MINSUNG** claps. Lights up.)*

NANHEE.
Wha–?

*(**MINSUNG** finds a condom.)*

Oh.

MINSUNG.
I am a responsible man.

NANHEE.
Yes.

(Clap, lights out.)

(Song continues and then erupts into bliss.)

MAN & WOMAN.
LA LA LA LA LA LA LA

MINSUNG.
Wow.

NANHEE.
That was nice.

MINSUNG.
Yes. Do you think it worked?

NANHEE.
I'm not sure.

MINSUNG.
Shall we turn on the lights?

NANHEE.
I'm nervous a little bit.

MINSUNG.
Me too.

NANHEE.
You too?

MINSUNG.
Surprisingly so. It's the first time I've worked so hard at sex for the appearance of my lady's father.

(**NANHEE** *laughs.*)

It feels great to be able to make someone laugh like that.

NANHEE.
It feels great to be made to laugh like that.

MINSUNG.
Your turn.

NANHEE.
What is.

MINSUNG.
To make me laugh like that.

NANHEE.
Okay. Are you ticklish?

MINSUNG.
Huh?

(**NANHEE** *tickles him.*)

That's cheating! Ah stop! Stop stop!

(Gunshot.)

(**NANHEE** *claps.*)

(Lights up.)

(There is a **PENGUIN HEAD*** *poking out of the toilet bowl.)*

PENGUIN HEAD.
I want my wings back.

MINSUNG.
Did it work? Is he here?

NANHEE.
No, I think, there's a penguin. In your toilet.

(**MINSUNG** *hits the flush and the* **PENGUIN** *is sucked into the toilet bowl.)*

---

*This should be voiced by the actor playing **FATHER**.

NANHEE.
Ho!

MINSUNG.
Is it still there?

NANHEE.
No. It's gone. I'm sorry. I'm probably just tired, seeing things –

MINSUNG.
Do you want to sleep over?

NANHEE.
Oh. Here?

MINSUNG.
I mean it's a tight space, you don't have to but,
you live so far from here and if you're tired, you are welcome to stay.
If you want.
Is what I'm saying?

NANHEE.
I would love to.

#7

(**NANHEE**'s *dream.*)

(North Korean military people with rifles march in singing the North Korean national anthem.)

(Somewhere, her **FATHER** *appears, or is it a* **PENGUIN***?)*

[MUSIC NO. 06 "NIGHTMARE I"]

CHORUS.
아침은 빛나라 이 강산
은금에 자원도 가득한
삼천리 아름다운 내 조국
반만년 오랜 력사에
찬란한 문화로 자라난 슬기론 인민의 이 영광
몸과 맘 다 바쳐서 이 조선 길이 받드세

PENGUIN.
Nanhee!

(Bang.)

(**PENGUIN** *falls.)*

#8

(Comic book room.)

MINSUNG.
Ta-da!

NANHEE.
It's, nice.

MINSUNG.
You've seriously never been to a comic book room before.

NANHEE.
I always thought comics were for children.

MINSUNG.
What?! No!! It's life. It's love. It's fantasy and reality rolled up into one dusty fluorescent room full of shelves upon shelves of awesomeness.
What?

NANHEE.
Nothing. It's cute. You are being very cute.

MINSUNG.
Oh. Sexy cute or emasculating cute?

NANHEE.
Definitely sexy cute.

MINSUNG.
That's what I thought.

CHORUS.
Brinng Brinng
Brinng Brinng.

MINSUNG.
It's my wife.

CHORUS.
Brinng Brinng
Brinng Brinng.

NANHEE.
Oh.

CHORUS.
Brinng Brinng
Brinng.

MINSUNG.
She hung up.

NANHEE.
Do you need to call her back?

MINSUNG.
No.
Do you mind?

NANHEE.
Go.

MINSUNG.
Sorry. I'll be right back, just, um, browse?

(A **PENGUIN** *appears.)*

NANHEE.
He is not real.

(Banpo Bridge.)

Ta-da!

MINSUNG.
It's nice.

NANHEE.
You've seriously never been to Banpo Bridge before.

MINSUNG.
Usually when I see the river I wish to jump in. And this bridge is notorious for such jumpers.

NANHEE.
That is a morbid thought for such a beautiful view.

(Bridge fountain show begins.)

It begins!

MINSUNG.
Oh wow that is so much water.

NANHEE.
200 tons of river, 380 nozzles, and 190 light fixtures will dance in rhythm and tempo, to delight and amaze. The world's longest bridge fountain, welcome to Banpo's Moonlight Rainbow Fountain Show!
What?

MINSUNG.
Nothing. You just, look very happy. It's a good look on you.

NANHEE.
Ah yes. I perform happy very well. That's how I get people to fall in love with me.

MINSUNG.
Oh. Am I falling in love with you?

NANHEE.
I don't know why I said that. Falling in love, I pick up South Korean idioms like lint to sweaters –

*(***MINSUNG** *kisses her.)*

Oh. Thank you. Good save.

MINSUNG.
Are you accusing me of kissing to divert from talking about the problem of love?

(A **CHORUS MEMBER** *makes a phone alert sound.)*

NANHEE.
Are you saying it wasn't a diversion?

CHORUS.

- HeeheeHeejin has uploaded four new posts on Instagram.

MAN.
Open app.

MINSUNG.
Do you wish to talk about the problem of love?

CHORUS.

- Image of Jimmy and your family in swimsuits.

NANHEE.
I think, I do?

CHORUS.

- HeeheeHeejin commented "church volleyball competition. #slayed" @JimKai.

MINSUNG.
Woh.

NANHEE.
But we don't have to talk about it if you don't want. It's okay.

MINSUNG.
(Distracted.) Okay.

MAN.
Three more images of Jimmy and your family in swimsuits.

*(**PENGUIN** appears.)*

CHORUS.

- Someone draft this girl for the Olympics @HeeheeHeejin.
- HeeheeHeejin commented: Thanks coach. @JimKai.
- Unimportantperson007 commented: Holy Shit Heejin is that your dad? #hot #sorrynotsorry.

MAN.
Close app. Delete app.

PENGUIN.
I'd rather fall into the river than fall in love with that guy.
Hey. I'm talking to you. Hey. I want my wings back.

(Riverbank.)

*(**MINSUNG** is teaching **NANHEE** to play "I Am Real" on his guitar.)*

MINSUNG.
It's D minor, A minor and then. F. That's a little bit harder.

NANHEE & MINSUNG.
하룻밤의 우리 소...

MINSUNG.
F.

*(**NANHEE** attempts F code badly.)*

NANHEE.
소...

MINSUNG.
F.

*(**NANHEE** attempts F code badly.)*

NANHEE.
소...

MINSUNG.
It's the –

NANHEE.
F! I know!

(She attempts F code badly. And again and again and again.)

MINSUNG.
Break?

NANHEE.
No! I am not the giving up kind.

MINSUNG.
I am worried I will lose my guitar to the water.

NANHEE.
Why?

MINSUNG.
You know, my phone, from before. I mean, it was a joke. It's okay.

NANHEE.
Okay.

MINSUNG.
What better place to learn songs than by the river? Where you can throw things in when frustrated?

NANHEE.
Is that still a joke?

MINSUNG.
Yes.

NANHEE.
Why do you keep making the same joke when I find it unfunny?

CHORUS.
Brinng Brinng
Brinng.

MINSUNG.
It's my wife.

NANHEE.
What does your wife have to do with your unfunny jokes?

MINSUNG.
Nothing. The phone call is from my wife. Nothing to do with my joke you didn't get.

PENGUIN.
Wow. That's kinda mean.

NANHEE.
(To self, re: Penguin.) Here we go.

MINSUNG.
What do you mean by that?

NANHEE.
What do you mean what do I mean?

MINSUNG.
Are you trying to pick a fight?

NANHEE.
No?

MINSUNG.
Then what did you mean about here we go, because it is not my fault that sometimes she calls, we have a child we have to care for together, whatever that means now, I can't apologize every time she calls, or every time you don't get my joke, none of those things are my fault?

NANHEE.
So don't?

PENGUIN.
Fight fight fight fight!

CHORUS.
Brinng Brinng.

PENGUIN.
Is it his wife again?

CHORUS.
Brinng Brinng.

PENGUIN.
It's his wife again.

CHORUS.
Brinng Brinng Brinng Brinng Brinng.

*(**NANHEE** takes **MINSUNG**'s phone and turns it off.)*

(Phone turning off.) Doorooroorooroooo.

MINSUNG.
I'll go umm, get some beers.

(He goes.)

NANHEE.
Go away.

PENGUIN.
I will when I get my wings back.

CHORUS.
• The account you're trying to reach is currently unavailable. Leave a message after the Peeeeeeeeeeeeeeeep.

WIFE.
I wish you would change your greeting.

Your voice is much nicer than the machine woman.

I am in Hartford. At the airport. Long-term parking lot.

Is it worth saying,
When I called, I thought, this is a phone call telling you to pick me up at the Incheon Airport.
But then the machine lady said you were unavailable.

And now, I don't know what to do Minsung.
People should talk to people.
Every day that I wake up alone on my little bed I think, people should talk to people.
And here we are talking to machine people
who repeat the same greeting every time you are unavailable
and we say it is for our child
it is for our child that you are unavailable, that I am unavailable
a spell I have cast on my brain,
every phone call missed, every flight cancelled,
every motion a married couple ought to not engage themselves in, has been okayed by the spell and has made me small. Made you small.
I don't want to be small anymore. I don't want to make you small anymore.

Heejin and I are moving to Texas.

With Jimmy.

I'm sorry.

CHORUS.
Peep peep peep peep peeeeep peeeeeeeeeeeeeep peeeeeeeeeeeeeeeeeeeeeeeeeeeep peeeeeee eeeeeeeeeeeeeeeeeeeeeeeeeeeeeeeeeeeeeeee/eeeeep.

NANHEE.
...But that's not the real ending of the story.

MINSUNG.
Hm?

*(**MINSUNG** and **NANHEE** are in a bed.)*

NANHEE.
In the original story, the angel goes back. Once a year. But my father, he left that part out. Why? Why do that?

MINSUNG.
Sorry what I wasn't listening.

NANHEE.
Why?

MINSUNG.
Because it's three a.m.

NANHEE.
Why would he change the ending? He didn't want us to return, right? If we made it to paradise, he wanted us to stay. He would never want his wings back.

MINSUNG.
What?

NANHEE.

The penguin that I told you about wants his wings back but obviously it's not my real father and the original ending is stupid because why would anyone do that? Because duh, who leaves paradise, just to see their family?

MINSUNG.

People who miss their family?

NANHEE.

Ha! I very nearly killed myself crossing three borders to get here.
Spent a whole year of my life tricking my tongue to speak differently.
Spent another three years, tricking my brain to think differently.
And now I work for the government.
Do you know how many defectors work for the government?
Do you have any idea how amazing it is that I made it to the place where I can serve orange juice and coffee to the cubicle workers of the South Korean Government?
Look at this face.
This is the face of the hero who has climbed over impossible walls to find success in paradise.
It is not the face of the idiot who risks paradise because she misses her family, no?

MINSUNG.

I love you.

NANHEE.

What? I was saying something. I was trying to tell you something.

MINSUNG.

Isn't this more important? That I love you? That I finally was brave enough to say I love you?

NANHEE.

Why is that brave?

MINSUNG.

Because. It is.

NANHEE.

You love me.

MINSUNG.

Yes.

NANHEE.

Okay.

MINSUNG.

Do you love me?

NANHEE.

No.

MINSUNG.

Oh.

NANHEE.

I don't know you. You don't know me.

MINSUNG.
Love isn't about knowing someone it's –

NANHEE.
It's what then. What is it about.

MINSUNG.
It's just, feelings, I have feelings, about you and I'm telling you.

NANHEE.
Feelings. Okay. You have feelings. What does that do?

MINSUNG.
What do you mean, what does it –

NANHEE.
If I have feelings with you too what does that do? Does it make my life better somehow, my life that is as meaningful as the tip of a toenail that is clipped off during a pedicure?

MINSUNG.
Why are you so upset?

NANHEE.
We are not together because of love. We are together because we are alone and being together paralyzes that terrible feeling for a while.

MINSUNG.
You know what forget it.

NANHEE.
You want this temporary paralysis to be love.

MINSUNG.
I said / forget –

NANHEE.
You hope that by saying this, "I love you," something is going to change, but nothing will change, the flame will die and that is just hope torture isn't it?

MINSUNG.
How are you so sure it will die?

NANHEE.
You're married. I am freezing to the color blue and you are running around shouting, "Look look we found one matchstick!!" But look around, where is the wood where is the coal –

MINSUNG.
What does that even mean? I just confessed my love. Who reacts like this to a confession of love?
What is wrong with you?

NANHEE.
Nothing is wrong with me! South Koreans are obsessed with love. I love. You love. All because of love. But then you find love, then you send them away to another country, and live alone in a closet with a shower hanging over it, / that is not real love.

MINSUNG.
Right because North Koreans so great at Real Love. You can't even tell your boyfriend, or in fact, your own father that you are escaping the country because he might report you and

you are probably never going to see him or anyone you ever "loved" ever again, and you can't give two shits about what you did to people you left,
what are you doing?

NANHEE.
Leaving.

MINSUNG.
This is your house.

NANHEE.
Keep it.

MINSUNG.
What? Don't be crazy.

NANHEE.
Do not call me crazy.

MINSUNG.
I'm getting a divorce.

NANHEE.
?

MINSUNG.
My wife. She is divorcing me. She has found a better man who can –
I'm sorry about – Sorry.
Stay.

NANHEE.
When?

MINSUNG.
Last week. She told me last week.

NANHEE.
Are you okay?

MINSUNG.
No.

NANHEE.
Are you crying?

MINSUNG.
No.
Maybe a little bit on the inside.

CHORUS.

- No new emails.
- No new messages.

MINSUNG.
I feel old and useless.

CHORUS.

- No new Facebook notifications. Refresh browser.

NANHEE.
Is that why? Why you said you love me?

MINSUNG.
Do you really feel like your life is as meaningful as the tip of a toenail that is clipped off during a pedicure?

NANHEE.
No. Sometimes.

MINSUNG.
It is not true. You have impact. You make me feel less old and less useless.

Do I have impact on you?

NANHEE.
Yes.

MINSUNG.
Couldn't we call that love, for now, and see what happens? Couldn't that be enough, for now?

NANHEE.
–

MINSUNG.
Okay. I take it back. I will feel the feelings only inside, and I cancel saying I love you. But when I find wood and or coal I will say it again.

NANHEE.
You know that it is not actual wood and or coal, it was a metaph–

MINSUNG.
Yes. Thank you. I know.

NANHEE.
I just had this image of you stacking up coal in your collapsible bed and confessing more love.

MINSUNG.
I won't. I promise.

#9

[MUSIC NO. 07 "NIGHTMARE II"]

(**NANHEE**'*s dream.)*

CHORUS (PENGUINS).

진짜라짜짜 진짜라니까 나

FATHER.

I was born in Pyongyang,

I have a wife, and six children. Four boys, two girls.

I was a flute player in the military band in Pyongyang,

but we relocated after an incident at my daughter's school where she asked a question about why the Fatherland isn't doing anything to get the buses running again.

(His head is dunked into a toilet bowl.)

CHORUS.

가짜라짜짜라니

(Head resurfaces.)

FATHER.

And we loved our relocation very much but then the daughter disappeared one day I don't know where she is.

CHORUS.

맘이 아파와

FATHER.

She was kidnapped. I am sure of it. She was ensnared in the clutches of a secret agent of the puppet government and dragged to South Korea. I am sure of it. I don't know where she is.

(His head is dunked into a toilet bowl.)

CHORUS.

진짜라짜짜짜 보라니까 진짜야

(And then resurfaces.)

(He has a penguin head.)

FATHER.

Every day in South Korea is a nightmare. It is a society of darkness, not only to the people like my daughter who has been dragged there, but to the South Korean people themselves.

(Gunshot.)

(His penguin head is blown off.)

To evil daughter who is subject to this humiliation, I implore you, come back to the Fatherland.

Come back to the Fatherland.

Come back to the Father.

I want my wings back.

(**NANHEE** *wakes up.)*

(She goes back to her Fatherland.)

#10

(**MINSUNG** *is on YouTube.*)

MINSUNG.
Hello everyone. My name is Guk Minsung.
I am a goose father.
My wife took our daughter and left me for a Japanese-American in Texas.
I have a lady.
She left me too.
She went back to North Korea to bring back her family and said that I should write a song for her if I get sad because that is what I did before and it helped.
It has been a month, since she left me a note on her side of my bed and disappeared.
So I wrote a song, in hopes it might help.
I don't think it will because I don't think they have YouTube in North Korea and writing songs only works when you believe that the person you wrote it for can hear it, but.
It's not terrible. The song. I used to be in a band so.
(Hello to my buddies from Pigskin Barbeque if you're seeing this.)
Anyways. Here's my song.

[MUSIC NO. 08 "I WANNA DIE"]

나나나
죽고 싶다이아이야
나나나
죽고 싶다이아이야
나나나
죽고 싶다이아이야
나나나
죽고 싶다

CHORUS.
- Park Jiyun likes this.
- Um Joosong likes this.

MINSUNG.
죽을만큼 그립지는 않아
죽을만큼 걱정되지 않아
죽을만큼 슬프지도 않은데
나나나 죽고 싶다이아이야

CHORUS.
- Kim Hanee / likes this.
- Kate Lim likes this.

MINSUNG.
나나나
죽고 싶다이아이야

CHORUS.
- Jin / likes this.
- June / likes this.

• John Park / likes this.

• Twenty-six shares.

MINSUNG.

죽었는지 궁금하긴 해 가끔

CHORUS.

• 1,067 views.

MINSUNG.

죽었으면 꿈에 나타나

CHORUS.

• Fritz / likes this.

• Kai / likes this.

• Zahir / likes this.

MINSUNG.

죽었다고 말해주라 나 지금

CHORUS.

• 5,300 / views.

• 181 shares.

MINSUNG.

나나나 죽고 싶다이아이야

CHORUS.

• Ping likes this.

• Kobe likes this.

MINSUNG.

나나나

CHORUS.

LIKE SHARE CLICK

MINSUNG.

죽고 싶다이아이야T

CHORUS 1.

• Call Mama if you get lonely sweetie.

• Dude's face at 1:56 is my screensaver LOL.

• This isn't real. North Korea is a closed country, god people are idiots.

• TBH mad addicted to this song.

CHORUS 2.

LIKE SHARE CLICK

LIKE SHARE CLICK

CHORUS.

LIKE SHARE CLICK SHARE THIS DON'T DIE LIKE SHARE CLICK SHARE THIS DON'T DIE
LIKE SHARE CLICK SHARE THIS DON'T DIE LIKE SHARE CLICK SHARE THIS DON'T DIE

CHORUS 1.

• This is so sad I was adopted from Korea so I know.

• Don't die!

• I'll totally sleep with you.

• Is this real?

• So sad. He's kinda funny though.

CHORUS 2.

LIKE SHARE CLICK (DON'T DIE DON'T DIE)
LIKE SHARE CLICK

LIKE SHARE CLICK (DON'T DIE DON'T DIE)
LIKE SHARE CLICK

CHORUS.

LIKE SHARE CLICK SHARE THIS DON'T DIE LIKE SHARE CLICK TAG THIS DON'T DIE SHARE THIS DON'T DIE

LIKE SHARE CLICK TAG THIS SHARE THIS DON'T DIE DON'T DIE

CHORUS.

- So real. Check him out on *Good Morning Seoul*. Click here to go to link.
- I totes wanna learn that dance for prom.
- Someone put him out of his misery ugh.

CHORUS.

LIKE SHARE CLICK (DON'T DIE DON'T DIE)
LIKE SHARE CLICK

LIKE SHARE CLICK (DON'T DIE DON'T DIE)
LIKE SHARE CLICK (DON'T DIE DON'T DIE)

CHORUS.

LIKE SHARE CLICK DIG IT DON'T DIE SHARE THIS DON'T DIE LIKE SHARE CLICK SHARE THIS DON'T DIE

LIKE SHARE CLICK DIG IT DON'T DIE SHARE THIS DON'T DIE LIKE SHARE CLICK SHARE THIS DON'T DIE

Like Share Click don't die.

MINSUNG.

63빌딩에서 날아볼까

CHORUS.

- Wife's a fucking cunt poor guy.

MINSUNG.

반포대교로 갈까

CHORUS.

- What you get for fucking a commie.
- 54 people like this.

MINSUNG.

사회 물의 끼치지 말고
청가사리 한두 사발 마실까 하 하

CHORUS.

- Jesus loves you stay strong.
- In bed.

MINSUNG.

육이오가 지난지가 언젠데

CHORUS.

- North Korean girls are Hot.
- Click here for hot Asian porn.

MINSUNG.

우리 여태 이 모양인가

CHORUS.

- I love K-pop. Please upload more vids!

MINSUNG.

나도 나도 나도 나도

CHORUS.

- I went to NK last year. Place is fucked up.

Like *Hunger Games* fucked up.

MINSUNG.

북한이나 갈까
북한이 나을까

• I find this video hilarious is that terrible?
No yes yes 1011.

CHORUS 1.	**MINSUNG.**	**CHORUS 2.**
• Kara / likes this.	북한으로 가면 니가 있나	0110 01001101
• JD / likes this.		
• Malachi / likes this.		
• 1,089 shares.		
	북한남과 눈맞았을까	01100100 11010110
LIKE LIKE SHARE 101 DON'T DIE.		01001101 01100100
	죽다 살아 나서 여기 왔는데	
YURI LIAM 011 LIKES THIS 1 DIE.		11010110
1011TAG 0 DIE.	왜 다시 죽으러 갔냐 이 가시나	01001101
		01001 01001
	야야야 죽고 싶냐이아이야	
0 IT LIKE 0 CLICK 10110 010010100		01001

CHORUS.
100,000-plus views.

MINSUNG.
죽을만큼 그립지는 않아
그치만 그리우니까
죽지 않았으면
집에 와

That's the song.
I hope you liked it. I hope you liked my song Nanhee, if you can see this.
I miss you, and I'm sorry I wasn't enough.

(He takes a gun to his temple.)

(Shoots.)

(A cute stream of water shoots into his face.)

Oh. I thought that would have more impact.

(He shoots a couple more times into the air.)

It's a water gun.
Just a little, performance art.
Um. Okay.
Pigskin Barbeque forever. Rah.

(End of video.)

#11

CHORUS.

- GooseGuy "suicide song" viral among teenagers and Hongdae dance venues.
- Students raise awareness for North Korean defectors at Yonsei University.
- GooseGuy signs contract with Melon.com for single of "I Wanna Die."
- Defector speaks out against MrGooseGuy's ignorance in his response rap, "So Die."

NANHEE.

Dear MrGooseMan,
I am home.
I found my father in the kitchen, making seaweed soup for his birthday.
He was so surprised to see me.
And so surprised to see all the money I brought!
He is keeping it safe until we figure out a plan to leave here for good.
For now, I am hiding in my childhood room.
It is smaller than I remember, this room.
It is not smaller than your *koshiwon.*
I wish I could send this letter to your *koshiwon.*
Sadly I can't because I am in North Korea and your *koshiwon* is not.
But maybe if I think my letters loud enough you will hear them.
I am sorry I left without saying goodbye.
But I will see you again so soon!
Don't feel old and useless.
From MinersDaughter.

P.S. There was never a phone.
Mister Lee was, as suspected, a son of a dicksquash and I wish him to hell
but I am glad my dreams were not real.

CHORUS.

- First snow of the year!
- It is only October our earth is dying. WAKE UP / PEOPLE!

MAN.

Minsung, what's on your mind?

CHORUS.

- Sunday Night Docu: Who was Yoo Nanhee? Lover or Spy?

MAN.

Where are you MrGooseMan? Thousands of elite women are waiting for your poke of love.

CHORUS.

- It's my first celebrity sighting! GooseGuy buying beers at 7-Eleven near Banpo Bridge.
- Attached: Picture of GooseGuy in pjs and sad hair.
- Retweet.
- Retweet.
- Retweet.

MAN.
Minsung, you have 747 new friend requests.
Are you sure you would like to deactivate your account?

MINSUNG.
Yes.

MAN.
Are you sure?

MINSUNG.
Yes I'm sure.

MAN.
But what if she tries to pm you through Facebook?
What if she tries to find you and you are a broken page for her?

MINSUNG.
Cancel account de-activation.

NANHEE.
Dear GooseMan,
He doesn't want us to cross over.
He wants to use the money for practical things, like food and clothing,
not certain death in the winter river.
Meanwhile, I am still imprisoned in my childhood room.
It's been a few months since I heard your voice.
Do you remember my voice?
Have you found a new friend to send emojis to?
If not, don't.
From MinersDaughter.

CHORUS.
- JINGLE BELLS JINGLE BELLS
- Holiday special movie of the past, watch *Home Alone Two* with your family on channel –

MAN.
Minsung! What are you doing for Christmas?

CHORUS.
- Do things!
- Buy things!
- Look at all these other people who are happier than you!

MAN.
Are you sure you want to log out of Facebook instead of stalking pictures of your family's new family on their first Christmas without you?

CHORUS.
- GooseGuy's daughter is a serious hottie. #Whosthedaddy? #4realztho link to pic.
- Retweet.
- Retweet.
- Retweet.

Five Four Three Two One.

MAN.

Minsung! What are you doing for New Year's?

CHORUS.

- Do things!
- Buy things!
- Look at more other people who are happier than you!

Bring bring bring bring bring bring bring.

MINSUNG.

Passport, die. Passport no good for going America.
They think my friend was an intelligence hazard, **Spy, For North Korea. Spy.**
no no **Spy No. Daddy Friend No Spy.**
But they just want me to be nearby when they have questions.
I would be on a plane right now if I could. I love Texas. I love you.
Could you come here for a week or so?
Whenever you want.
No no don't give the phone to your mother I can –
Hi.
I just thought, For a week or so.
I am sorry I am such an embarrassment.
Will you –
Will you just, put my daughter back on the phone.
Will you put our daughter back on the –

CHORUS.

- Disconnected.

NANHEE.

The penguins are gone, and the father is real,
And I thought that was all I ever wanted.
It turns out, not.

CHORUS.

Tick tock tick tock tock tick tock tick.

NANHEE.

Hey, remember when I came to your *koshiwon* and
demanded sex for the appearance of my father?
I wish there was a way to demand the appearance of you, right now.

CHORUS.

Tick Tock Tick Tock Tock Tick Tock Tick.

NANHEE.

Should I just swim across the river without a broker or my father?
I don't know if I have it in me to swim across any more rivers Minsung.
I feel old and useless.
Hellloooooo. Can you hear me?

MAN.

Minsung, you have –

CHORUS.

- No new emails.
- No new messages.
- No new Facebook notifications.

NANHEE.

I am thinking a thousand letters to you like your poke-type messages.

CHORUS.

- Students raise awareness for something else at Yonsei University.

NANHEE.

But I feel crowded with my own voice and cannot remember yours.

CHORUS.

- Someone else's something else viral among teenagers and Hongdae dance venues.

MAN.

Guess our fifteen minutes are up, huh?

NANHEE.

I cannot even remember some parts of your face.

CHORUS.

- Heejin Cook is not available to chat.

NANHEE.

I miss your *koshiwon*, the smell of floor wax.
Your voice,
I miss, you.

MAN.

What's on your mind?

NANHEE.

Love, Nanhee.

MAN.

Minsung, what's on your –

(Gunshot.)

CHORUS.

- One-hit wonder Guk Minsung found with a gunshot wound in his Shinchun *koshiwon*.
- Alleged suicide of Guk.
- Alleged assassination of Guk.
- Goose fathers, how bad is it really?

NANHEE.

Dear Minsung,
I saw your YouTube song about wanting to die.
(Please don't die.)
My father found it in the black market.
He asked me if I was your lady.
I said, yes. I also said you are getting a divorce.
He shook his head but I could see him smile a little

as he opened a jar of alcohol
and when we were both dizzy with warmth
I finally told him about my dreams with the penguins
and he laughed and laughed
and he said
fathers never want their wings back.
And then he lifted the floorboard he was sitting on
and gave me the exact amount of money that I gave him when I first arrived.
He did not spend any of it.
And he said
go,
fly.
I will see you so soon.
Your Nanhee.

CHORUS.
- Nation mourns the death of beloved GooseGuy with a candlelight vigil.
- Guk Minsung; a life.
- Guk Minsung; a death.
- Guk Minsung's life to be made into a blockbuster starring Song Kang-ho.

MINSUNG.
Hi, this is Guk Minsung. Thanks for calling but I can't come to the phone right now. Leave a message after the –

CHORUS.
PEEP.

HEEJIN.
Hi Dad.
I just called to say hi.
I never did that, I think. Call to say hi.
Okay bye.

MINSUNG.
Hi this is Guk Minsung. Thanks for calling but I can't come to the phone right now. Leave a message after the –

CHORUS.
PEEP.

HEEJIN.
Hi Dad.
Just came back from your funeral.
They didn't let Mom in but they let me in so I put a flower by your photo.
I wrote my name on the stem so you would know which was mine.
I wrote it in Korean. Guk. Hee. Jin. Looks like a five-year-old wrote it but,
Um.
Okay bye.

MINSUNG.
Hi this is Guk Minsung. Thanks for calling but I can't come to the phone right now. Leave a message after the –

CHORUS.
PEEP.

HEEJIN.
I got into UT. It's short for University of Texas.
It's a pretty big deal. Mom and Jimmy bought me a car. Prius.
Um. Your phone gets disconnected tomorrow.
I'm glad I got to tell you I got in.
Um.
Okay. Bye.
Um.
Actually. I also want to say, because I don't know where else to say,
Um.
I'm really angry, I think.
I can't forgive you for this.
I didn't really know you. I know I was a bitch to you. So I am sorry.
But now I have to be sorry forever.
I don't know how to –
Um.
Okay bye.

CHORUS.
• The number you are trying to reach is no longer in service. Please try again.

NANHEE.
I'm back.
Like I said I'd be.
It took a long time.
Like I said it might.
I just wanted to say that I think what you did was very stupid.
I saw your YouTube video.
You look very handsome.
I like your song.
I am sorry it didn't help.

CHORUS.
• The number you are trying to reach is no longer in service. Please try again.

#12

*(**NANHEE** at Banpo Bridge, alone in the crowds.)*

*(Next to her is the **PENGUIN**, nicely dressed up in a very penguin-like tuxedo.)*

(They look at the bridge fountain.)

PENGUIN.
Are we waiting for the fountain?

NANHEE.
No. It's winter. They shut it down for the winter.

PENGUIN.
Then what are we doing here?
Are we waiting for spring?
Are we waiting for you to stop feeling like a tip of a toenail that is clipped off during a pedicure?
Are we waiting for him?

NANHEE.
He's dead.

PENGUIN.
Your mind can re-create fathers, penguins, father-penguin hybrids in varied states of terrifying.

NANHEE.
I don't mind this version too much.

PENGUIN.
Thank you. Me too. Don't evade. I'm just saying, you could probably re-create other things if you wanted.

*(**NANHEE**'s mind makes the bridge fountain begin!)*

Oh nice. But I meant the other, other thing.

MINSUNG.
Leave her alone. Maybe she's not ready to see the other, other thing.

NANHEE.
Oh.

PENGUIN.
Yay you did it!

MINSUNG.
Your penguin's back.

PENGUIN.
I was just leaving.
*(To **NANHEE.**)* I'll be right here if you need me sweetie.
*(To **MINSUNG.**)* You. Don't fuck it up.

(He gives them some space.)

MINSUNG.
*(Re: **PENGUIN.**)* You really need some new friends.

NANHEE.
Why did you [do it?] –

MINSUNG.
Oh you know, I was lonely.
Did you find him? Your real dad?

NANHEE.
Yes.

MINSUNG.
Was it nice to see him?

NANHEE.
Yes.

MINSUNG.
Did he want his wings back?

NANHEE.
No. If nothing else I have helped you understand metaphor.
My life has had impact. It is not completely meaningless.

MINSUNG.
Thank you for your impact.

NANHEE.
Thank you for yours. I'm sorry we didn't get to call it what you wanted to call it.

MINSUNG.
Maybe it's not too late. Do you still have it?

(Magic sounds. **NANHEE** *pulls out a match.)*

NANHEE.
Oh. It's so nice.

MINSUNG.
Very. Are you thinking you could take our very nice very pretty match to light it with some new guy?

(This makes **NANHEE** *laugh.)*

Coz I'm okay with that. I can be okay with that. Eventually.

NANHEE.
Thank you. But this one is for you.

(She lights the match.)

*(***MINSUNG** *claps. All the lights go dark.)*

I will miss you. For a really long time.

MINSUNG.
Thank you.

(He kisses **NANHEE** *on the head.)*

NANHEE.
Go. Fly.

*(***MINSUNG** *leaves the light.)*

(Alone, **NANHEE** *lets the glow of the flame fill her up with hope.)*

(Then, gently, she blows out the match, like a kiss to his heart.)

(Goodbye.)

End of Play

ENGLISH TRANSLATIONS

#4: I Am Real

I AM REAL
YOU SAY I'M NOT REAL MAKES ME SAD
REAL BREATHING
REAL FEELINGS
REALLY REAL COME SEE, I AM REAL

WHY DO YOU DOUBT ME
WHY DO YOU LAUGH AT ME
WHY TRY TO FORGET ME
AND OUR VERY PRECIOUS ONE NIGHT
WHY DO YOU HATE ME
EVERYONE HATES ME
I'LL BE BETTER
ONE MORE NIGHT, GIVE ME
ONE MORE CHANCE

I AM REAL
YOU SAY I'M NOT REAL MAKES ME CRY
REAL HEART
REALLY BEATS
REALLY REAL COME SEE, I AM REAL

#6: Nightmare I

SHINE, MORNING ON THIS RIVER AND MOUNTS
FULL OF RESOURCES, SILVER AND GOLD
THREE THOUSAND MILES OF BEAUTY IS MY MOTHERLAND
A LONG HISTORY OF FIVE THOUSAND YEARS
GLORIOUS ARE THE WISE PEOPLE BRED IN CULTURE
LET US SERVE OUR CHOSUN WITH BODY AND HEART

#7: Nightmare II

I AM REAL
YOU SAY I'M NOT REAL
REAL MAKES ME SAD
REALLY REAL. COME SEE I AM REAL.

#8: I Wanna Die

I I I
WANNA DIE
I I I
WANNA DIE
I I I
WANNA DIE
I I I
WANNA DIE

NOT DYING TO SEE YOU
NOT DYING OF WORRY
NOT DYING OF SADNESS
BUT I I WANNA DIE

I I I
WANNA DIE

WONDER IF YOU'RE DEAD SOMETIMES
IF YOU ARE, COME TO MY DREAMS
TELL ME YOU ARE DEAD COZ

I I I WANNA DIE
I I I
WANNA DIE

SHOULD I FLY FROM 63 BUILDING
TAKE A TRIP TO BANPO BRIDGE
OR DON'T BE A SOCIAL NUISANCE
CHUG A BOWL OF ACID INSTEAD HAHA
BEEN SO LONG SINCE THE WAR
HOW ARE WE STILL STUCK IN THE SAME PLACE

SHOULD I I I I I I I ALSO
GO NORTH TOO?
WOULD IT BE BETTER?
IF I GO NORTH WILL YOU BE THERE?
HAVE YOU FOUND A NORTHERN MAN?

YOU SURVIVED SO MANY DEATHS TO BE HERE
SO WHY
DID YOU GO TO DIE, STUPID GIRL
HEY HEY HEY
DO YOU WANNA DIE

NOT DYING TO SEE YOU BUT
BUT I DO MISS YOU, SO
IF YOU DID NOT DIE
COME HOME.